Discard

AIRCRAFT

AIRCRAFT

by Alan Dahnsen

An Easy-Read Fact Book

FRANKLIN WATTS
New York | London | 1978

Cover by Gail Gibbons

Library of Congress Cataloging in Publication Data

Dahnsen, Alan.
  Aircraft.

  (An Easy-read fact book)
  Includes index.
  SUMMARY: Describes the characteristics and
different uses of a variety of aircraft including bal-
loons, dirigibles, gliders, and airplanes.
  1. Airplanes—Juvenile literature. 2. Air-ships—
Juvenile literature. [1. Airplanes. 2. Airships]
1. Title.
TL547.D15   629.133   77-15092
ISBN 0-531-01351-0

Airplanes are an important part of our lives. They take people, cargo, and mail from one place to another. They travel faster than cars, trains, ships, and buses. They can cross land or water.

The 747 is the largest **passenger airplane**. It has **jet engines** and is called a jumbo jet. This airplane has room for about 350 passengers and 16 crew members. It can fly across the United States in just 5½ hours.

Airplanes carry cargo as well as passengers. Mail is often carried in the **baggage compartment** of airliners. So are small packages that must arrive quickly. Some medicines (MED-uh-sins) and food are sent by air, too.

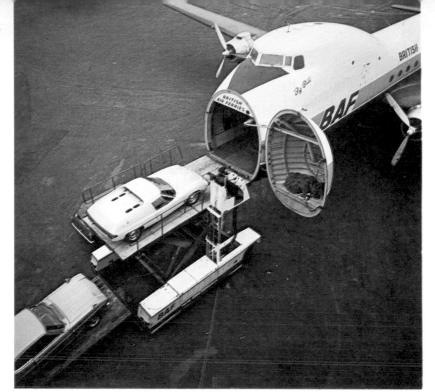

Special **cargo planes** carry large, heavy things.
This kind of plane has a long, wide **hold** (cargo area).
It is big enough to carry cars and machinery.
Its front end opens like a large door.

Airplanes can help to save lives. Someone who is sick and lives far from a doctor can be taken quickly by air for medical help.

Some farmers use planes to dust their crops. They can cover a lot of land in a short time. Dusting with chemicals (KEM-uh-kuls) kills weeds and insects that destroy crops.

Viggen

Draken

Mirage

Fighter planes are used by the air force. They are much smaller than passenger or cargo planes. They are also much faster. They can fly faster than the speed of sound. The word for the speed at which they fly is **supersonic**.

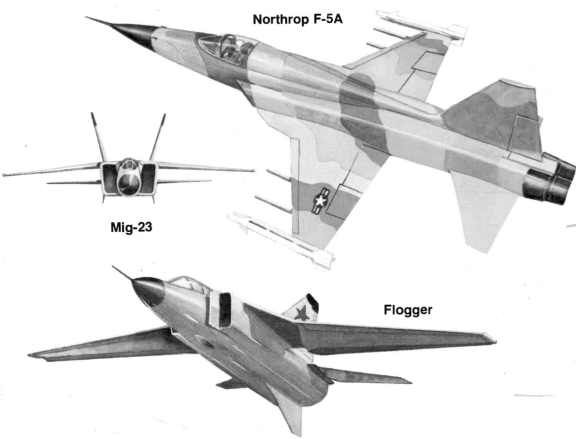

Northrop F-5A

Mig-23

Flogger

Sound travels about 1,087 feet (331 meters) per second. Supersonic planes can travel more than twice the speed of sound.

11

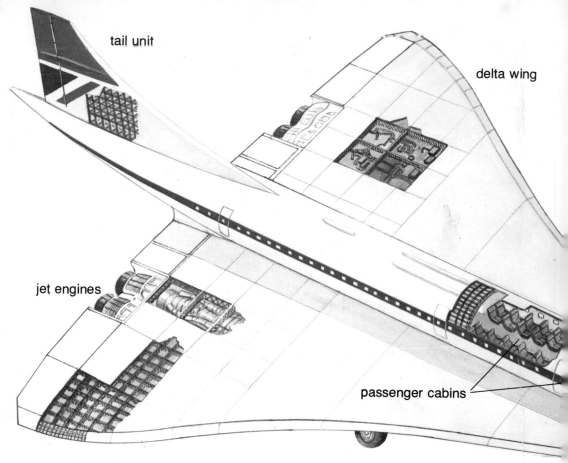

tail unit

delta wing

jet engines

passenger cabins

In 1976 the first supersonic passenger plane
began to fly between Europe and the United States.

The **Concorde** is a supersonic plane. It saves travel time. But it uses much more fuel than slower planes. It also makes much more noise.

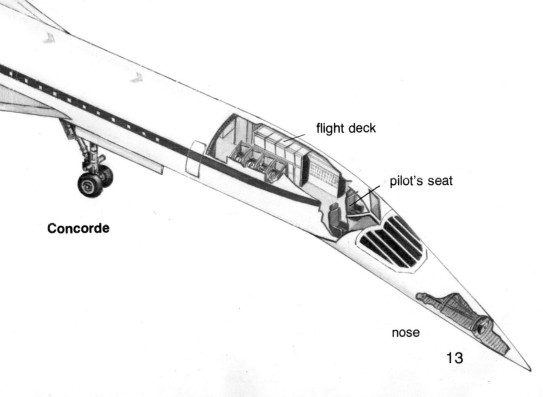

flight deck

pilot's seat

Concorde

nose

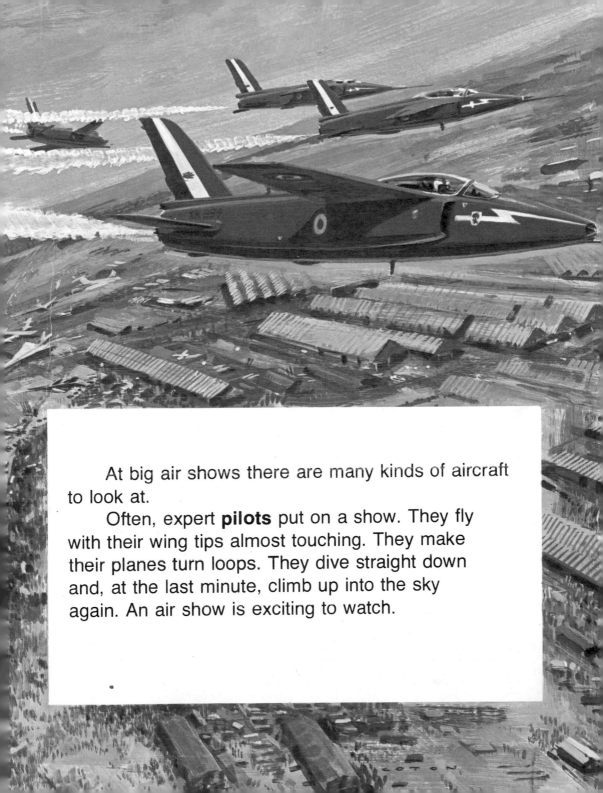

At big air shows there are many kinds of aircraft to look at.

Often, expert **pilots** put on a show. They fly with their wing tips almost touching. They make their planes turn loops. They dive straight down and, at the last minute, climb up into the sky again. An air show is exciting to watch.

sailplane

Gliders are aircraft without engines. Some are also called **sailplanes**.

A glider has to be towed into the air by a plane with a motor. When it gets up high, the glider is let go. The glider pilot rides on air currents and guides the glider back down to the ground.

Seaplanes have **floats** instead of wheels. They can land and take off on water.

A plane called an **amphibian** (am-FIB-yun) can take off and come down on water or land. It has a body like the **hull** of a boat. There are wheels in the hull so it can come down on land.

Most planes need to go a long way to
take off. They have to move along the ground until
they are going fast enough to lift into the air.

VTOL (VEE-TEE-OH-ELL) planes do not need a
long run to take off. VTOL means "vertical takeoff and
landing." VTOL planes lift straight off the ground.
The engines push these planes straight up on takeoff
and let them drop straight down when landing.

The **helicopter** is another kind of VTOL. It has
rotor blades that lift it off the ground.

The rotor blades of a helicopter spin like the blades of a fan. The pilot can change the **angle** of the blades. Changing the angle makes the helicopter go forward or back, up or down. It can even make the helicopter stand still in the air. Helicopters are sometimes called **choppers**.

Most aircraft are heavier than air. They need engines to give them **power** to fly.

The very first aircraft was lighter than air. It was a **balloon**.

A balloon is a large bag filled with special gas, or hot air. It goes up because the gas or hot air in the bag is lighter than air. It has a basket under the bag for the pilot to ride in.

A **blimp** is lighter than air, too. But it has an engine that the pilot uses for steering. A blimp is also called a **dirigible** (DIR-uh-juh-bul).

Wings are a very important part of a plane. At one time, many planes had two wings on each side, one above the other. Today most planes have one wing on each side.

The main job of the wings is to lift the plane into the air. Wings have a special shape that makes this possible.

The top side of the wing is more curved than the under side. The air flowing across the top moves faster because it has to go farther. The air flowing under the wing goes slower in an almost straight line. The fast-moving air presses less. The slow-moving air presses more. It moves up against the wing and lifts the plane.

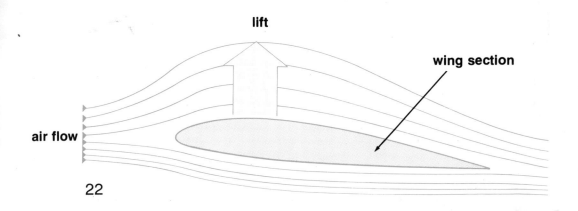

lift

wing section

air flow

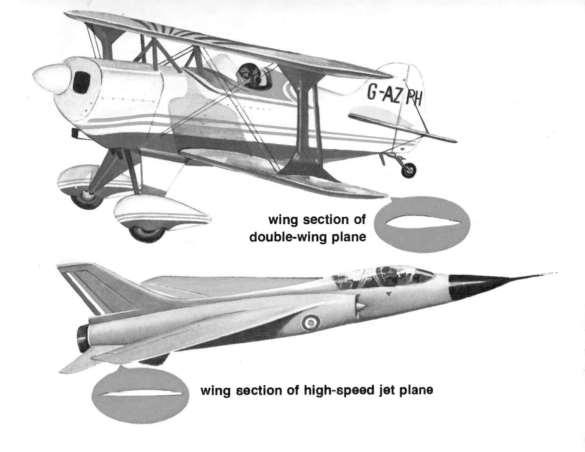

wing section of
double-wing plane

wing section of high-speed jet plane

The faster a plane moves, the more the slower air presses up.

A plane moving through the air causes **friction** (FRIK-shun). Another name for friction is **drag**, which slows the plane. The **streamlined** shape of a plane cuts down on drag. The smooth form and pointed nose help the plane to move quickly. The less drag there is, the faster the plane can fly.

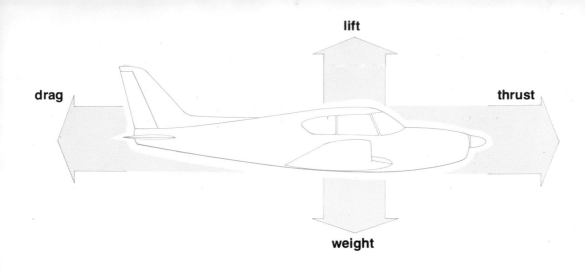

lift

drag

thrust

weight

Thrust is the force that pushes a plane through the air.

In some smaller planes thrust is made by a **propeller**. The plane's engine makes the propeller turn.

in-line piston engine

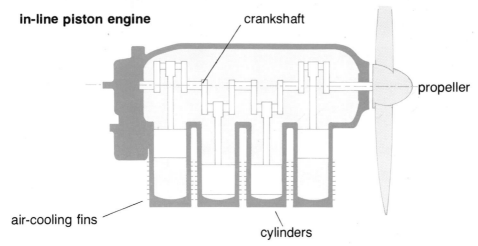

crankshaft

propeller

air-cooling fins

cylinders

horizontally opposed piston engine   **radial piston engine**

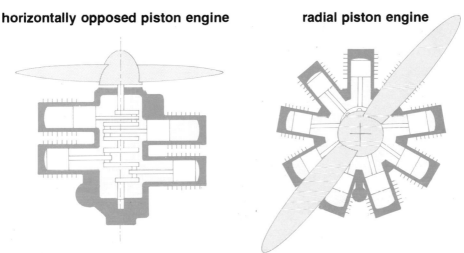

A plane that is driven by a propeller has a
piston engine. This kind of engine has pistons
that move up and down in **cylinders** (SILL-in-durs)
and turn the propeller.

A piston engine uses **gasoline**.

Today most large planes have jet engines.

To get an idea of how a **turbojet** engine works, think of what happens when you blow up a balloon and let it go without tying the end. The balloon rushes forward as air pushes out of the open end.

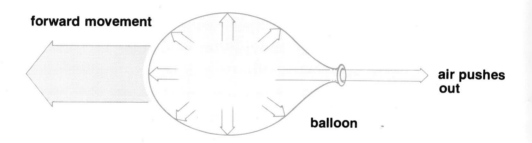

forward movement

air pushes out

balloon

This drawing shows how the same kind of thing happens in a turbojet engine.

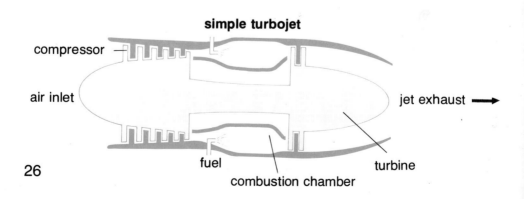

simple turbojet

compressor

air inlet

jet exhaust ➡

fuel

combustion chamber

turbine

A **compressor** pulls in air and pushes it into **combustion** (com-BUS-chun) **chambers**.

The air and fuel burn to make hot gas. The gas pushes through the **turbine**, making it turn as the air moves out of the engine.

two-shaft turbojet

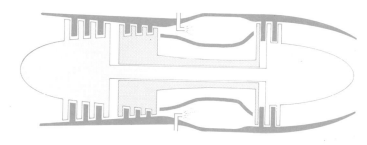

turboprop

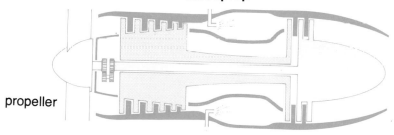

propeller

In a **turboprop** engine, the turbine drives a propeller to give the plane thrust.

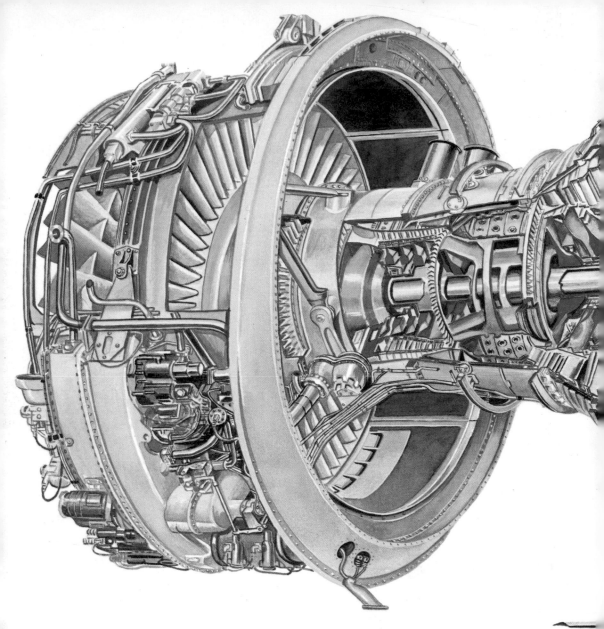

This large engine is a Rolls-Royce RB-211. It is used in the Lockheed Tristar airliner. It gives a thrust of 42,000 pounds (19,000 kilograms).

Lockheed Tristar

29

Piper Comanche

Every plane has a **tail**. The tail is important because it helps to keep the plane steady when it is flying.

A plane is always pushing against air as it moves. That makes the nose of the plane move up and down, which is called **pitching**. The **horizontal** part of the tail, the **tail plane**, keeps the plane from pitching.

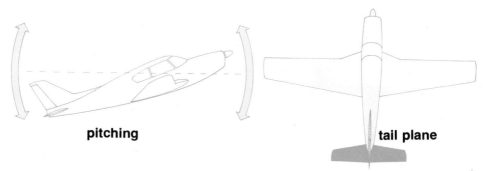

pitching   tail plane

The **vertical** part of the tail, the **tail fin**, keeps the plane from swinging from side to side, which is called **yawing**.

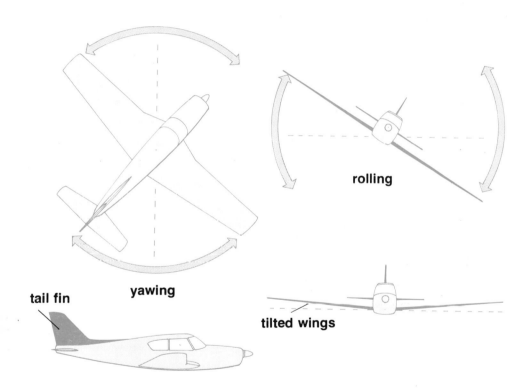

rolling

tail fin

yawing

tilted wings

The wings of the plane are tilted up at a slight angle to keep it from rocking from side to side, which is called **rolling**.

The pilot has to be able to make the plane turn, and move up or down. This is done by moving the **control surfaces** on the wings and tail. The main control surfaces are the **ailerons**, the **elevators**, and the **rudder**.

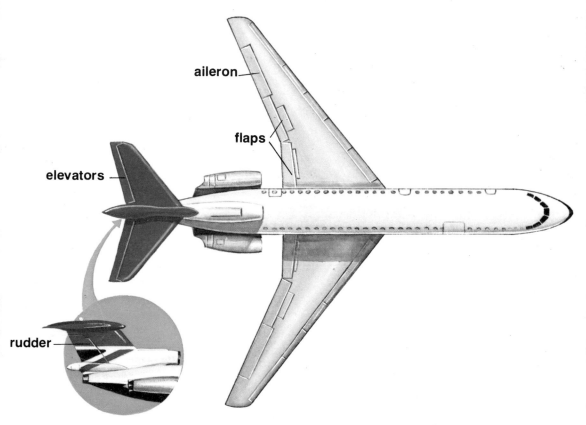

aileron

flaps

elevators

rudder

The ailerons are at the back of the wings, near the wing tips. Moving the ailerons tilts the plane. This is called **banking**. This makes turning easier.

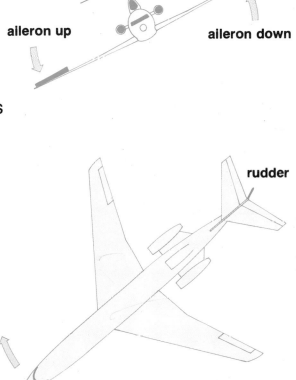

elevators

aileron up

aileron down

rudder

The elevators are at the back of the tail plane. Moving them pushes the plane's nose up or down.

The pilot controls the ailerons and elevators with a steering handle called a **stick**.

The rudder is at the back of the tail fin. Moving it pushes the plane's nose to the left or right. The pilot moves the rudder by foot pedals.

Flaps are other important control surfaces on the wings of a plane. The pilot lowers the flaps just before landing. This helps the plane to land gently.

Very important when landing, of course, are the plane's wheels. They are called **landing gear**. They go up into the plane's body while it is in the air. They are lowered just before landing.

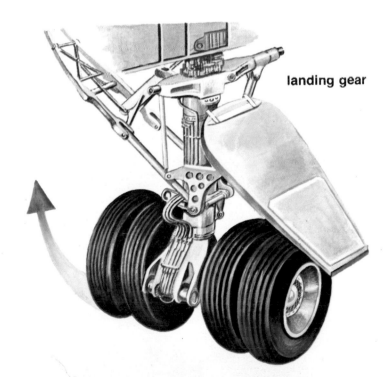

landing gear

In the early days, pilots could fly only during the day when the weather was good.

Today's planes have all sorts of **instruments**. Now planes can fly during the day or night. They can fly in good or bad weather.

A **compass** shows if the plane is heading in the right direction.

The **altimeter** (al-TIM-uh-ter) shows how high the plane is flying.

The **air speed indicator** shows how fast the plane is moving.

All these instruments, and many more, help to make flying safe and comfortable.

instrument panel on Concorde flight deck

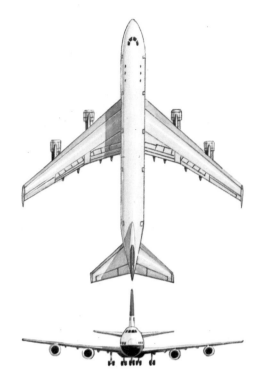

Lockheed Hercules
flying speed 366 miles per hour
          (590 kilometers per hour)

Boeing 747
flying speed 590 miles per hour
          (950 kilometers per hour)

    Planes are not all the same. The size and shape
of a plane depend on how it is to be used, what
it will carry, and how fast it must go.
    A cargo plane is large but not fast. A fighter
plane is small and very fast.

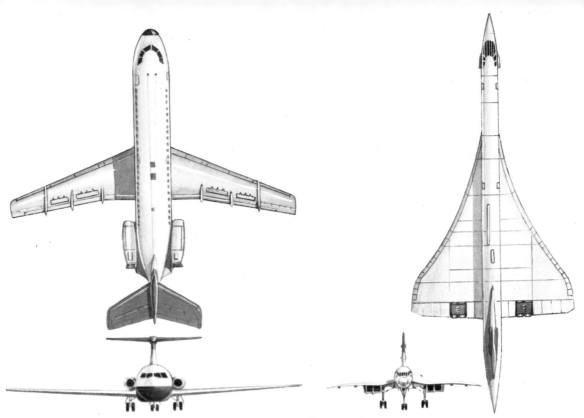

BAC One-eleven
flying speed 540 miles per hour
              (870 kilometers per hour)

Concorde
flying speed 1425 miles per hour
            (2300 kilometers per hour)

Planes that fly very fast have wings that are swept back at an angle. The streamlined shape cuts down on drag. Planes that fly slower have straight wings.

The people who design aircraft begin by making a small **model**. They try out the model in a **wind tunnel**. They take pictures of how the air flows around the model.

The test helps them to know how a full-size plane will work in the air.

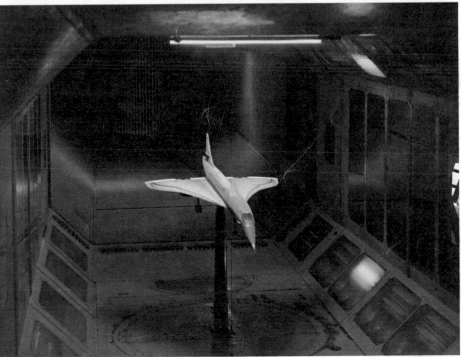

After many models are tested, the aircraft company picks one as the best design. Then all the plans for that model are made larger for a full-size plane.

Designers make drawings of each part of the plane.

making the parts

testing the parts

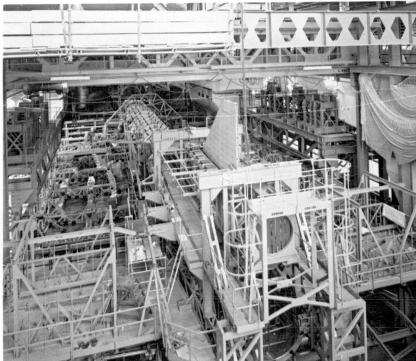

The drawings show how to build each part. Then **engineers** test the parts to make sure they work perfectly. The engine must run smoothly. The instruments must be accurate. The body and wings must be strong.

After all the parts are tested, a full-size trial model is made. A trial model is called a **prototype**.

The prototype is tested. If it works well, the aircraft company sets up an **assembly line** to mass produce the plane.

New airplane designs are being tested all the time. Designers and engineers keep trying to make planes that are safer and faster.

The plane of the future may fly people non-stop around the world in a few hours.

SMOKING
PROHIBITED
IN THIS
DEPARTMENT

tarom

tarom
ROMANIAN AIR TRANSPORT

SUPER ONE-ELEVEN

45

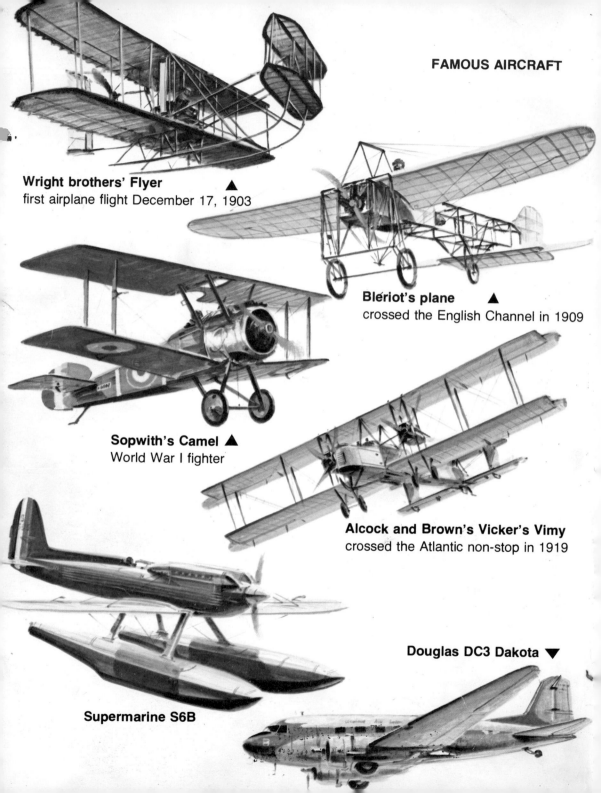

FAMOUS AIRCRAFT

Wright brothers' Flyer ▲
first airplane flight December 17, 1903

Blériot's plane ▲
crossed the English Channel in 1909

Sopwith's Camel ▲
World War I fighter

Alcock and Brown's Vicker's Vimy
crossed the Atlantic non-stop in 1919

Supermarine S6B

Douglas DC3 Dakota ▼

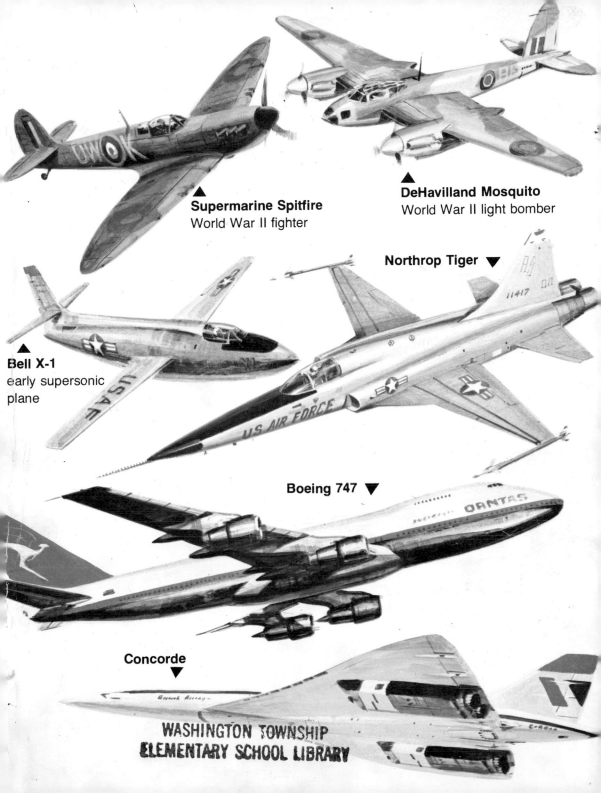

Supermarine Spitfire
World War II fighter

DeHavilland Mosquito
World War II light bomber

Northrop Tiger ▼

Bell X-1
early supersonic
plane

Boeing 747 ▼

Concorde
▼

Index